THE
PROBLEM SOLVING
POCKETBOOK

By Jonne Ceserani

Drawings by Phil Hailstone

D1393386

Published by:
Management Pocketbooks Ltd
Laurel House, Station Approach, Alresford, Hants SO24 9JH, U.K.
Tel: +44 (0)1962 735573   Fax: +44 (0)1962 733637
E-mail: sales@pocketbook.co.uk
Website: www.pocketbook.co.uk

This edition published in 2003. Reprinted 2004, 2006.

© Jonne Ceserani 2003

British Library Cataloguing-in-Publication Data – A catalogue record for this book is available from the British Library.

ISBN-13   978 1 903776 04 9
ISBN-10   1 903776 04 X

Design, typesetting and graphics by **efex ltd**   Printed in U.K.

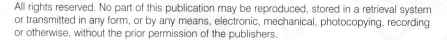

CONTENTS

AUTHOR'S NOTE

The Synectics problem solving structure and the core tools for using it are also described in *Big ideas, putting the zest into creativity and innovation at work*, published by Kogan Page. *Big ideas* is a leadership book describing a range of perspectives about leadership style, behaviour, values, beliefs and tools for managing these in a commercial world.

This pocketbook is a handy reference workbook that focuses entirely on problem solving and the tools and techniques to raise your probability of success. While some of the ideas are repeated you will find numerous examples of how to use the tools in this book, not available elsewhere.

1NTRODUCTION

A SERIES OF PROBLEM SOLVING MEETINGS

I regard life as a series of problem solving meetings, particularly business life. Think about it. Almost everything you do requires the same basic steps:

- Imagine a possible future
- Think about some ideas to achieve this (existing and/or new ideas)
- Make some choices
- Refine the choice to establish a solution
- Take action

You may do this on your own or with others, therefore the meeting may be in your head or involve huge groups of people. It may be completed in an instant, almost a reflex, or it may take years.

It does not matter because the underlying process is always the same. This is great! It means that being good at solving problems is a life skill that will often help you to be successful.

A SYSTEM OF BEHAVIOURS, TOOLS & TECHNIQUES

Forty years ago two people in a design invention team became curious about why it was that on some days they had productive problem solving sessions and on others the group argued a lot and went round in circles.

They began to videotape the meetings and review the behaviour of the group. They noticed recurring behaviours, some very useful and constructive, others very destructive.

They decided to try and change how they organised and behaved in meetings, doing more of the constructive things and finding new ways of managing the destructive behaviour. They were successful and became more effective by their measures. The two men also began to wonder if they could make creativity and innovation more than just an *accident*.

"Did I say that?"

3

A SYSTEM OF BEHAVIOURS, TOOLS & TECHNIQUES

SYNECTICS

They created a new word, **Synectics**. The word is derived from the Greek *syn*, the bringing together of diverse elements, and *ectos*, from outside. This ongoing research has given birth to a growing body of knowledge concerned with collaborative effort focused on problem solving.

From continued observation of problem solving invention and design sessions across a broad spectrum of industries, a set of tools and structures has been developed which allows people to improve their probability of success when using the processes of creativity, eg:

- Having ideas
- Being creative when you want to be
- Making choices when looking for new ways of working
- Developing new solutions from the kind of woolly ideas people first come up with when speculating about possible futures

These tools and processes are used in many major international firms across the globe.

PERCEPTIONS THAT PROMOTE PROBLEM SOLVING

IF YOU BELIEVE

IF YOU BELIEVE YOU WILL SOLVE A PROBLEM THEN YOU WILL.

Trite words, or a truth about life?

Listen to a sportsman, sports commentator or coach. In snooker, for example, when a player is not performing well you will hear people saying, 'His mental game is not there'. Players talk about being *in the zone*, meaning being in a mental state that includes believing in success.

For some reason many of us regard this as obvious for sport, but completely fail to attach any importance to the same idea at work. Successful problem solving begins with framing - perceiving the issue or task in an appropriate way that will lead us to success.

HALF EMPTY OR HALF FULL?

You will have heard the expression: *Is the glass half empty or half full?* Are you someone who thinks of life pessimistically as half empty, or optimistically as half full?

How you think about a problem will change the chemistry of your brain as it prepares itself to fight, or defend, etc. Thinking *half full* tends to make problem solving easier.

For those of you who have been on a course and heard that *all problems are opportunities*, this is fine providing you genuinely believe it. If you just use the words nothing will change.

What follows in this section are some models and thoughts giving you useful ways to think about the world to aid problem solving.

CYCLING WORLDS

OPERATIONAL WORLD

You spend most of your time in an **operational world**.

It is a world associated with carrying out routine activities, in learned or programmed ways. You base your decisions on procedures or rules and expect to experience successful outcomes, which you normally do.

- Driving a car is a common example: mostly you arrive at your destination in one piece
- Working on a production line is associated with a repetitive set of processes that uses a common set of inputs to manufacture a stream of identical products
- Office administrative procedures are another example of routine activities

CYCLING WORLDS

OPERATIONAL WORLD

The operational approach is a focused blinkered way of working, which is perfectly fine providing you continue to experience successful outcomes.

What are you to do if existing solutions, and any known alternatives, begin to fail?

What if you experience success and also see that new opportunities could be identified?

You need a different way of working. You will have to cross over into the **innovation world**.

This is a place where you will suspend your normal way of working and behave very differently.

CYCLING WORLDS

INNOVATION WORLD

Speculative exploration is necessary in order for something new to be imagined.

Year in, year out, the moon shines in the sky. One day someone must have looked up and acknowledged this.

'I wish I could visit the moon. I wonder how I could do that?'

Someone has to speculate to provide a view into a possible future, so that you can have an idea and engage in some idea development.

'I know, cannons fire projectiles. I'll build a large cannon. It doesn't work. Firework rockets may be the answer. I will build a large rocket. Still doesn't work but it does mean a lighter object can be made to travel through space like a cannon ball. Clearly this needs further ideas ....'

Speculate

Develop solution

Innovation cycle

Experiment

Constructive review

CYCLING WORLDS

INNOVATION WORLD

You could have been that person. You speculated, had an idea, and tried it as a possible solution.

Clearly, since it does not work, you will need further activity to **refine or modify** the idea.

Then you can try some further **experimental action**.

In order to learn from failure you will want to engage in **constructive evaluation**.

This cycle of activity is dramatically different from the operational world, which is associated with tunnel vision and focus on task to the exclusion of other interference. The innovation world needs an open mind, and fun-loving childlike behaviour.

OH GOODY LET ME LET ME!

CYCLING WORLDS

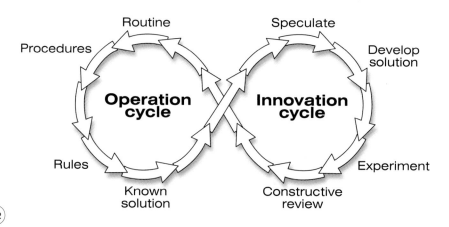

CYCLING WORLDS

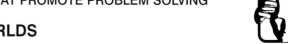

In a business these two worlds are constantly in conflict:

●   Operational thinking is about **now** and **knowing the answer**
●   Innovative thinking is about **the future** and **not knowing**

If we make suggestions to you, when we are in innovation mode, about how you can run your business differently, and you are thinking operationally, you will be able to tell us why none of our suggestions will work. You will probably be right as well, and the conversation will be pointless.

PERCEPTIONS THAT PROMOTE PROBLEM SOLVING

REFRAME YOUR THINKING

Reframing is the process of taking a situation and thinking about it from different perspectives. A paradigm shift is an example of a reframe. Lucozade was a drink for ill people, now it is a health drink.

If you have a problem that needs solving, it is because your thinking is stuck, so unstick it using **metaphors or analogies**. This is also fun, which helps the climate in a useful way, as you will read shortly.

Telling people you are feeling a bit pressured may describe your problem but it does not sound much when framed that way. Telling them you feel the weight of the whole world pressing on you is more graphic, ridiculous, a metaphor and all the more powerful for being so.

In framing an issue, the more graphically you can help people visualise the task and get a feel for the emotion and energy that go with it, the more likely you are to identify and work on the real issue.

MANAGING RISK & THE CAPACITY TO EXPERIMENT

You have probably read slogans developed for total quality programmes, eg:

Do it once, do it right
Right first time

The same companies that adopt these slogans also often say about themselves: we are *risk takers*, and *our employees are empowered to experiment with new ideas* (providing they get it right first time, of course!).

We know a company that tried to spread all four of the messages above, usually in the same breath. The messages are contradictory and belong in different worlds.

In the operational world it is appropriate to expect people to perform a task correctly and to make a minimum of errors. It is about doing what we know, in a way we understand, for a predictable outcome.

You now know that it is impossible to enter the innovation world unless you are able to speculate, and experiment.

MANAGING RISK & THE CAPACITY TO EXPERIMENT

MANAGING RISK & THE CAPACITY TO EXPERIMENT

Real risk is when it actually hurts if you fail. If you jump off a cliff there is a real risk you will get hurt when you hit the ground.

Emotional risk is the nervous feeling of excitement you have when you are not sure about an outcome, like stage-fright.

● **Gamblers** take real risks. Consistent losses lead to bankruptcy. Gambling is exciting, therefore highly emotionally charged. Gambling is a place where it is important to know the outcomes so that you can measure the risk, the odds

Not a safe place for innovation.

● **Clerks** operate in routine ways, delivering routine known outcomes

Not a safe place for innovation.

17

MANAGING RISK & THE CAPACITY TO EXPERIMENT

- **Ostriches**, by tradition, operate with their heads buried in the sand. This is a dangerous place to be. It feels safe, yet danger may lurk nearby. The entrepreneur, possibly an engineer with an acclaimed new product he produces from his garage, may feel very successful. However, although an excellent engineer, his skills do not include finance, so he is not aware of growing receivables that are taking him towards bankruptcy. He is amazed when the bank manager arrives to foreclose on his mortgage.

Not a safe place for innovation.

- The **experimenter** is able to innovate, take risks, make mistakes, fail, and continue. An experimenter is safe because he or she is minimising the real risk of failure, while the excitement of learning and experimenting provides the energy and drive to continue.

If you set out to develop a new explosive it is best done in a test tube. The mistakes will be survivable.

ROLES & RESPONSIBILITIES
(ACCOUNTABILITY!)

DON'T BLAME THE REFEREE

PROBLEM OWNER

There are only three roles needed for a meeting, no more, and it is important to get the roles sorted out in order to raise the probability of success in your meetings.

Two of the roles are derived from a job normally undertaken by a single person, the person chairing the meeting. These two roles are better shared between two people.

The first role is **problem owner**. This is assumed by the individual who is **accountable** for the results of the meeting, who should also be the **decision maker**, and who is responsible for the **direction** of the meeting, since only he or she can know where it needs to go.

There is almost always only one problem owner although sometimes when you ask the question, everyone raises a hand. If this happens, ask who gets fired if things go wrong. Usually only one hand is left. This is an important issue for problem solving. The reason many groups are so poor at problem solving is because the task of making someone accountable has never been sorted. Once you have a committed owner the problem solving becomes a lot easier.

DON'T BLAME THE REFEREE

FACILITATOR

Problem owner is a *content* role focused entirely on problem solving, getting ideas, sorting things out and finally making the decisions.

This is possible because of the second role, **facilitator**. The facilitator is the referee. He or she does not kick the ball, ie: have ideas, and does not take part in the content of the meeting. The job is to manage the *process* of the game so that the players keep to the rules, make progress and score goals (make decisions).

Facilitators are responsible for designing the meeting, managing the communication and ensuring the climate remains conducive to success.

ROLES & RESPONSIBILITIES (ACCOUNTABILITY!)

DON'T BLAME THE REFEREE

RESOURCES

The third role is that of **resource**. Resources are people invited to the meeting to have opinions and ideas, when they are asked for them. They have a responsibility to shut up when the problem owner has to decide.

Resources are sometimes confused because they think they are decision makers when they are not. I once worked with a company that had virtually ground to a halt because nobody would let anybody do their own job. Everyone tried to interfere and get involved in decisions that were not theirs to make.

Resources come in a range of categories:

- **Implementers** - A problem owner wanting commitment to his/her decisions is wise to involve implementers so that they contribute to the decision (not make it!)

- **Barriers** - The people whose support is needed to get the decision made, and will also be important after the decision has been taken. If they are part of helping to reach the decision, commitment will be built

DON'T BLAME THE REFEREE

RESOURCES

Categories continued:

- **Experts** - Problem solving needs ideas and the expertise to bring ideas together in order to create solutions. Experts clearly have a part to play

- **Non-experts** - Naïve resources who know nothing about the problem often have the most interesting ideas. Unlike the experts, they are prepared to guess and don't worry about making mistakes. Often the breakthrough comes outside the main stream of thought, the Dyson vacuum cleaner being a recent example

ROLES & RESPONSIBILITIES (ACCOUNTABILITY!)

WINNING COMMITMENT

(AND OVERCOMING THE *NOT INVENTED HERE* SYNDROME)

When you are working on your own you do not expect winning commitment to be an issue. This may be true in terms of reaching a solution but what happens when you try to implement your solution? People prefer to work on their own ideas in preference to yours. Often their energy will be directed towards telling you why your idea won't work, rather than helping it to succeed.

Guidelines for making decisions
- Be sure you can carry it through
- Give people a chance to understand why you are making this choice
- Work hard to build commitment later, and continue with this
- Don't assume commitment is a steady state

WINNING COMMITMENT

(AND OVERCOMING THE *NOT INVENTED HERE* SYNDROME)

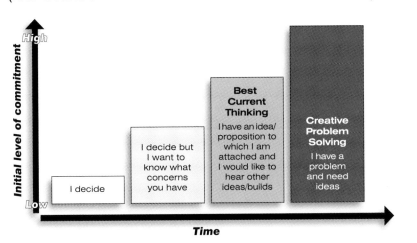

25

WINNING COMMITMENT

(AND OVERCOMING THE *NOT INVENTED HERE* SYNDROME)

- **I decide** is the fastest way to get to a solution but results in very low levels of commitment from others

- **I decide and want to hear your concern** begins to address involving others. Most people will accept *No* if they understand why and know they have been listened to

- **I have an idea and want to involve you in reaching a decision** will build much higher levels of commitment and is the beginning of problem solving. Best current thinking (BCT) is a useful construct, and is described in detail later

- **Creative problem solving** builds the highest level of commitment. For *creative* you can equally read *open minded*. They are the same things in terms of the ways you will work while problem solving

Notice the left axis in the foregoing diagram reads *initial level of commitment*. Commitment quickly dies unless you work hard to maintain it.

WINNING COMMITMENT

(AND OVERCOMING THE *NOT INVENTED HERE* SYNDROME)

A story to encourage you to problem solve

As you move to the right on the bottom axis of the diagram (page 25) the time taken to reach a decision increases. The issue becomes how much time and money you will save in the future if you have the willing commitment of others.

My favourite quote from a client is that we helped them accomplish nine months' work in three days. The event in question was a three day problem solving session. The client had an urgent need to create a series of personal product ideas in order to remain competitive. The session included a cross-section of people from the company including marketing, sales, R&D, finance, HR and even a Board member. Also included were external agencies, packaging designers and customers.

The single event was time-consuming to create and run. It was a high price! However, the pay off was much faster progress, products getting to market quicker and everyone's energy directed towards success. The cost saving was huge!

NOTES

BEHAVIOUR &
ORGANISATIONAL CLIMATE

BEHAVIOUR & ORGANISATIONAL CLIMATE

HELPFUL IDEAS & TOOLS

This section introduces a series of ideas and tools that you will find helpful in order to:

- Establish and maintain climates/cultures to support problem solving
- Get ideas
- Make choices
- Evaluate results
- Take action

USING YOUR ENERGY PRODUCTIVELY

FIELD & CLIMATE

- Field is what you generate around you with your personality, climate and the sum of the group's individual fields, the culture

- If you live in a climate where your life is constantly under threat, you will spend much of your time and energy thinking about self-defence and how to preserve your life

- If you set out to sail across an ocean to another land your activities will be focused on sailing the boat, plotting a course and enjoying the experience

USING YOUR ENERGY PRODUCTIVELY

FIELD & CLIMATE

- When the boat hits an old wreck and starts to sink, your focus will change and all of your energy will be directed towards the immediate task of staying alive

Businesses are like this. In order to move into an innovation world, essential for problem solving, you will need to consider your climate, or culture.

USING YOUR ENERGY PRODUCTIVELY

FIELD & CLIMATE

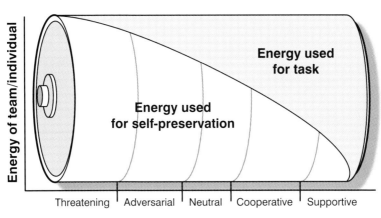

USING YOUR ENERGY PRODUCTIVELY

SELF-PRESERVATION

An individual, or team, has a certain amount of energy to give to doing some work. We are like batteries, containing a finite amount of energy. When the energy is all gone we will fall over and sleep or die.

If you operate in an *adversarial* or *threatening* way, or if this is how people behave towards you, your energy, or that of the team, will be directed towards self-preservation.

Adversarial behaviour includes:

- Pulling rank
- Failing to pay attention or listen to others
- Ignoring someone
- Cross-examining opinions with challenging questions

Threatening behaviour includes:

- Discounting or putting down other people's opinions
- Openly challenging ideas
- Reacting negatively or cynically to other people's views
- Preaching and moralizing
- Anger and threats of violence

USING YOUR ENERGY PRODUCTIVELY
CO-OPERATION

The innovation world can only thrive when you strive to operate in a positive climate.

Working co-operatively or supportively removes the need for self-protection, and team members are able to focus on the task and success.

The open, childlike, playful mind needed for innovation can only blossom when the need to defend yourself has been removed. It is also a more pleasant place to be, for you and your colleagues. And you get more work done.

USING YOUR ENERGY PRODUCTIVELY

POSITIVE BEHAVIOURS

Increases chances of success

Be optimistic
See the value in
Focus on what's going for the idea
Assume valuable implications
Seek to understand another's perspective

Be attentive
Listen
Be interested
Show approval
Acknowledge
Credit

No early evaluation
Jump to favourable conclusions
Set up win/wins
Make it *no lose*
Protect vulnerable beginnings

Take on faith
Temporarily susped judgement
Assume it can be done
Share the risk
Accept
Connect with
Join
Be open to/available
Build on it
Speculate along with

Listen approximately
Paraphrase
Deal as an equal
Eliminate status/rank
Give up all rights to punish/discipline
Support confusion
Value the learning in mistakes
Use ambiguity

USING YOUR ENERGY PRODUCTIVELY

NEGATIVE BEHAVIOURS

Be pessimistic
Preach/moralize
Be judgemental
Be critical
Disapprove

Take away from
Pull rank
Get angry
Scare

Act distant
Be inattentive
Do not listen
Do not join
Use silence against
Place burden of proof
Ask questions
Give no feedback
Be noncommittal
Put on a stony face
Be impatient
Nit-pick
Interrupt
Be bored
Assume no value
Make no connections

Reduces chances of success

Set up win/lose outcomes
Make fun of
React negatively
Discount/put down
Be cynical/sceptical
Insist on early precision
Correct
Point out only flaws
Misunderstand
Disagree before listening
Habitually argue
Constantly challenge

Be dominant
Command
Order
Direct
Threaten/warn
Demand
Blame
Make fun of
Be competitive

37

DISCOUNTING
REVENGE CYCLES

I am sure you can recall plenty of occasions when you have been in a meeting and have watched two people verbally sniping at one another. One criticises the other; from then on that second person looks for an opportunity to get them back!

This often develops into a game of tennis, each attempting to score points over the other. These *revenge cycles* sometimes continue over years. Revenge cycles are poor ways to use energy.

DISCOUNTING
NEGATIVE EFFECTS

Often this *discounting* of another person's opinions and ideas is unintentional. Sometimes a remark just slips out. In the vast majority of cases, the intention of the speaker is to be helpful and therefore positive. But the effect on the listener can be very negative. Given that this is the case, it is difficult for the discounter to change their behaviour because they do not recognise that they are generating effects that they do not intend.

As the person feeling offended after being discounted, you can **choose to let the effect on you be positive rather than negative** and get into a co-operation cycle.

Energy

Revenge Cycle

DISCOUNTING

HOW TO ASSUME POSITIVE INTENT

Next time you feel you are being criticised, try this technique. Respond with something like: 'Clearly we see things differently. I would be interested to share areas of agreement and explore where we differ.'.

You will need to find a form of words that you are comfortable with. The interaction that follows will be dramatically different from your normal experience.

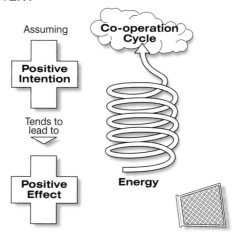

Assuming

Positive Intention

Tends to lead to

Positive Effect

Co-operation Cycle

Energy

DISCOUNTING

PRACTICE MAKES PERFECT

Get into a pair or group of three with some friends or colleagues. One of you begins to talk enthusiastically to the other(s) about a recent experience that was really exciting, powerful or emotional.

The other(s) should discount the speaker as many times as possible.
There are three ways to do this:

- **Oral** – Oh, what rubbish!
- **Tonal** – Oh, yes? (said in an obviously cynical tone)
- **Non-verbal** – Yawning, looking at your watch

You will find that you are really good at this. Many of us discount a lot, often without realising we are doing it. Discuss the effect this is having on one another.

USING (MISUSING) QUESTIONS TO HELP (HINDER) PROBLEM SOLVING

When a group of people gathers in a room to do some problem solving, and the problem owner describes the problem, almost without exception the participants will begin to ask questions. They want more information so that they fully understand the problem.

This wish for more information is positively meant. The participants want to be able to help the problem owner; therefore they wish to understand the problem. The unintended result is that they end up in the same hole as the problem owner, having acquired a set of blinkers similar to his.

USING (MISUSING) QUESTIONS

GETTING OUT OF THE HOLE

Think about how you feel when operating in a fog of misunderstanding. The answer is, probably, that you feel highly uncomfortable because you may get it wrong.

The problem owner can be pictured as a person in a hole in the ground. They are surrounded with so much information they are unable to see any new directions to move in.

A group, unencumbered with all this information, has the possibility of offering new perspectives. Members of the group can pass down a ladder offering access to new thoughts and possibilities.

(43)

USING (MISUSING) QUESTIONS

A STORY

Earlier we identified the role of *resource*. Naïve resources, that is, naïve about the task, can become a very important element in a creative problem solving group. Experts get in the way in the early stages because they think they know; knowing is what expertise is about. Clearly if the task needs problem solving they do **not** know.

Naïve experts open up new perspectives. Within your organisation it widens the audience that can be invited to participate in helping the business solve problems. You can mix technical, finance, HR, admin, marketing, etc because a naïve resource does not need knowledge.

I once ran a session exploring new opportunities for a novel food process. Customers were invited to the session although it was highly technical. The experts were forced to rethink how they described the ideas and, as a result, new perspectives were introduced. The customers were not allowed to ask lots of questions, they were encouraged just to guess.

USING (MISUSING) QUESTIONS
PUTTING PEOPLE ON THE DEFENSIVE

Some questions are asked for quite legitimate reasons, in the sense that they are questions asked with a genuine wish for the answer. Reasons for asking questions can be:
- To seek information
- To clarify
- To help others to participate
- To give someone an opportunity to demonstrate their expertise

Other questions lack this legitimacy, in that they are designed to demonstrate your personal superiority, or someone else's stupidity. For example:
- Asking a question you know someone can't answer
- Asking a question just to divert the discussion
- Asking a question to show off your own knowledge

You may not use all of these reasons yourself; you will know the ones you use and why. However, it is clear that questions are used for many purposes.

USING (MISUSING) QUESTIONS
PUTTING PEOPLE ON THE DEFENSIVE

You may have had the experience where someone has asked you a question, listened to your answer, and replied: 'No, no! That's not what I meant at all.'.

Apparently you have got it wrong, and you are left feeling stupid and defensive as a result. You have been discounted!

What has actually happened in this example is that you (the respondent) guessed the wrong option from that long list of reasons why questions are asked. You gave the right answer to the wrong question, and were made to feel bad because of it.

BEHAVIOUR & ORGANISATIONAL CLIMATE

USING (MISUSING) QUESTIONS

PUTTING PEOPLE ON THE DEFENSIVE

Feeling bad is an inappropriate state in a climate that is designed to nurture trust and innovation. If you are going to ask a question in your meetings, say what is behind the question and take away the need for guessing.

By being explicit about the answer you are seeking, you are more likely to get the right answer. If your question was actually for the purposes of checking out the feasibility of an idea, your colleagues will actually get to hear the idea, and ideas are essential for problem solving.

BEHAVIOUR & ORGANISATIONAL CLIMATE

USING (MISUSING) QUESTIONS
HIDING IDEAS BEHIND QUESTIONS

A colleague of mine was running an innovation session where the problem concerned a scum that formed on top of a brew. This fell into the brew and destroyed the flavour. Someone asked the following question: 'What temperature does the vat operate at?'. The problem owner gave the answer as so many degrees and the session continued.

During a break the questioner was overheard talking to a colleague. He was saying what a pity it was about the vat temperature because, given an increase of x degrees, a chemical could be used that would form the scum into a biscuit that could be lifted off.

The problem owner became excited, saying that the vat temperature was not that critical and could be changed so that the chemical could be used.

The idea was there all the time but did not get into the innovation session because the resource asked a question instead of giving an idea.

How many ideas exist in you and your organisation that are hidden because questions are asked instead of ideas being given?

BEHAVIOUR & ORGANISATIONAL CLIMATE

MANAGING IDEAS, DECISIONS, OPINIONS, FACTS

Problem solving is almost by definition a confusing activity. If you were not confused you could probably solve the problem. The probability of successful problem solving can be dramatically raised if you look for opportunities to sort out the confusion.

- Opinions
- Facts
- Ideas
- Decisions

These four words represent a key area for confusion.

Someone speaks with such authority that what they say must apparently be *fact*, therefore beyond doubt and unchangeable. Yet you have a problem. More often than not, what is really being expressed is only an *opinion* that could be changed, or maybe it is just an *idea*.

When I tell you what I plan to do it sounds like a *decision*. If it is one that you do not like, you argue with me. Actually, I was only sharing an *idea* but it sounded more definite than that.

MANAGING IDEAS, DECISIONS, OPINIONS, FACTS

BEST CURRENT THINKING (BCT)

Best current thinking (BCT) is, by definition, a statement of ideas and/or opinions that can be developed and changed. By being clear about this you help set a supportive meeting climate and establish a calm meeting with high levels of listening and co-operation. This is more likely to lead to successful problem solving.

BCT is also a way to short cut the problem solving process. If you come to a meeting with an early hypothesis for the group to evaluate and build on, it can speed things up, providing the group are clear it is just a hypothesis which can easily be rejected. Later in the book, we will talk about appropriate ways to evaluate early ideas.

As you move towards problem resolution with a large group it can be faster to share the BCT with the group, let them evaluate it and contribute new ideas, and then go away and develop the thinking in a smaller group. This is much faster and means everyone can participate, to build commitment, yet you can still work quickly.

LISTENING FOR IDEAS

Remember the last time you drove somewhere and could not consciously recall covering a particular stretch of road, driving on autopilot. Our minds have an enormous capacity to wander off on mental flights of fancy.

I imagine you can recall a number of occasions in meetings when you have suddenly realised you are not paying attention. As people are speaking, or delivering endless PowerPoint slides, your mind is stimulated in all sorts of directions, most of them seemingly little to do with the subject matter.

On such occasions, you probably wonder what has prompted your thoughts. Sometimes you will be embarrassed by what you are thinking.

LISTENING FOR IDEAS

Once your mind had been stimulated you will tend to give your attention to this meeting in your head, often more interesting than the public one in the room. You drop out. Your attention wanders (or wonders).

LISTENING FOR IDEAS

HOW EDUCATION DESTROYS OUR CAPACITY FOR IDEAS

People speak far slower than your mind can process thoughts, a factor of 10 or 12 being the difference.

This means that when someone is speaking in a meeting your mind has the capacity to generate thousands of thoughts and ideas. It is one reason why a problem solving group should be no larger than eight. Processing all of the thoughts becomes a major challenge.

At school you were taught to pay attention in order to understand. This is one way of listening that has value when you need to understand.

But problem solving needs **ideas**. Your natural listening pattern of dropping out and acknowledging the thoughts in your head is an essential part of successful problem solving.

IN-OUT LISTENING

INDULGE IN CHILDLIKE BEHAVIOUR

Next time you are in an ideas session let your mind wander and play games. Use whatever thoughts come to mind to stimulate ideas. A technique called **in-out listening** will help you manage the meeting in your head so that you can use your mind for ideas

BEHAVIOUR & ORGANISATIONAL CLIMATE

IN-OUT LISTENING
TEMPLATE FOR TRACKING IDEAS

- Divide a page of your notepad into two columns. The left hand column is for lecture notes. The right hand side is for jotting down any thoughts, associations, connections, images, etc. Draw pictures here too if you wish.
- When you are listening to the public meeting, make lecture notes
- When your attention level falls and you are listening to your private thoughts, make notes in the right hand column
- The trick to learn is to avoid censorship and record your first thought, whatever it happens to be. Often these thoughts may be ridiculous, impossible, rude, illegal or immoral. Try to avoid *improving* them; gather the first thought. You do not have to share it; that will be your choice

This technique also helps to overcome any tendency you may have to forget what it was you wanted to say, and it avoids the need to interrupt other people.

IN-OUT LISTENING

TEMPLATE FOR TRACKING IDEAS

ME:
Notes of
my own
connections,
images,
associations,
thoughts and
ideas

MUST BE PROFITABLE

QUALITY IS IMPORTANT

MUST BE SAFE

HIM/HER:
Lecture
type notes
of what the
speaker is
saying

SPEAKING TO MAXIMISE COMMUNICATION

WHY NOBODY HEARS YOU

When giving our ideas or opinions, most of us pack the important content in unnecessary baggage. We give a detailed introduction that leads up to the idea gradually, then express the idea itself, followed by with a summary of what we have just said. It is a response to the fact that we so often have our ideas discounted. We like to get the retaliation in first!

Many people are at their lowest level of attention just when you are telling them your main point. This might explain why there is so much misunderstanding in meetings.

SPEAKING TO MAXIMISE COMMUNICATION

HEADLINE & BACKGROUND

Here is a different approach to raise the level of communication.

Begin with a *headline*, a sentence that captures the core of the idea. Follow with *background*, words that tell people about the connections you made. This will in turn stimulate ideas in others who are using *in-out* listening. Forget the sell, it just wastes time in the meeting.

SPEAKING TO MAXIMISE COMMUNICATION

HEADLINE & BACKGROUND

Example:

Headline: how to make glass by floating it on water

Background: I was doing the washing up and I noticed how the grease floated on the surface as a beautiful, thin, even film which is just what we want for glass

Many of you may know that glass is made, not by floating it on water, because it explodes, but by floating it on molten tin. Alexander Pilkington was the man who had that idea.

EVALUATION

ITEMISED RESPONSE (IR)

Think about how you respond when new ideas or opinions are presented to you, and how others respond when you have ideas. **Itemised response (IR)** is a process for protecting ideas.

Speculation and new ideas are like snowflakes, easily destroyed unless you protect them. Given the right environment within which to grow and develop, stunning results can be achieved, like an ice hotel! But often groups evaluate ideas by saying only what is wrong, and the level of criticism, or evaluation, is so general that it cannot serve as a guide to how the thinking needs to be improved.

The IR process itemises, as a series of headlines, the evaluation of an idea or set of circumstances.

BEHAVIOUR & ORGANISATIONAL CLIMATE

EVALUATION

ITEMISED RESPONSE (IR)

Start half full.

- Begin by **listing the pluses** (positive aspects) of the idea. Potentially valuable thinking is frequently not recognised as such because insufficient time is given to working through the pluses of the idea. Looking for positives is, in itself, a building process

- Use **in-out listening** to trigger additional pluses and suddenly an idea can blossom

- After you have listed the pluses, consider **areas of concern** that need addressing (note: do not think of these as *what is wrong*). List these issues as headlines, using problem solving language like:

  - *How to…*
  - *I wish…*
  - *I need a way…*

This is the language of possibility, which establishes a problem solving mindset.

BEHAVIOUR & ORGANISATIONAL CLIMATE

EVALUATION

IR: POSITIVE FRAMING ON THE DRAWBACKS

If you believe something is impossible and simply say so, you leave very limited options for where to go next. *Impossible* is a shut out. Many members of the group will simply stop thinking about implementing the idea.

Turning this into a more positive focus will dramatically change the perspective of the group. Maybe you are thinking, 'I like the solution **and** my issue is:
- how to overcome trade union concerns
- how to swallow my own pride and agree
- I need a way to get others to agree
- I wish we could find cheaper labour'.

All of these statements are versions of *impossible* type thinking. They are more specific, however, are statements of *possibilities*, and we can now address the issues using problem solving.

EVALUATION

IR: PULLING THE RING-PULL CAN

Remember when you had to open a can of drink by using a separate can opener to create two holes? The ring-pull can tried to change all this by giving you a self-contained package which could be opened without a separate piece of equipment.

If you try listing all the things wrong with the original ring-pull can you will manage to produce a long list of faults, some apparently real show-stoppers. You drink from a dirty surface, it is not re-sealable, and children can cut themselves, for example.

You could be forgiven for wondering why the idea ever got off the ground. This was one of the most successful packaging concepts launched for years, yet if you start assessing why it **won't** work it is easy to kill the idea off.

So many companies fail to act because they scare themselves to death and never make the decision. Analysis paralysis again.

When looking at concerns, differentiate between **major** and **minor**.

EVALUATION

IR: A STORY

I once watched an excellent decision being wrecked by evaluation. The problem owner had made a major decision, and was looking very pleased with himself, deservedly. His colleagues were equally supportive of the decision.

Someone suggested using an itemised response to check the quality of the decision. On the face of it, a perfectly good idea. The group generated four flipcharts of headlines describing the positive features of their choice and everybody was looking even happier.

OK so far!

EVALUATION

IR: A STORY (Cont'd)

They then began to list issues and concerns; I knew there were none of any major significance that would change the decision. It was silent for a while. Eventually the first very very minor concern was raised. This was followed shortly by a second, which opened the floodgates to other even more minor concerns.

As the list grew, I watched the energy in the group visibly change, and went in to stop the meeting before the process caused even more damage.

EVALUATION

IR: A STORY (Cont'd)

What was going wrong was that the group failed to acknowledge that there were no major concerns. The decision was a good one and should simply have been allowed to go ahead. The minor concerns raised by the group were of no consequence in terms of affecting the decision actually made. Many were simply imagined possible issues that might never happen.

In problem solving it is often better simply to go ahead and try something, and then see what the real issues are that arise.

(The pure itemised response, used in isolation as an evaluation tool, calls for listing **all** major concerns before problem solving to resolve the concerns. This differs from the process used during the ideas development phase, once you are engaged in problem solving, where the process calls for identifying and resolving **one** concern at a time. See page 113 for an explanation of this difference.)

PLANNING

WHICH WAY?

'Cheshire puss,' she began rather timidly... 'would you tell me please which way I ought to go from here.'

'That depends a good deal on where you want to get to,' said the cat.

'I don't much care where,' said Alice.

'Then it doesn't much matter which way you go,' said the cat.

'So long as I get somewhere,' said Alice as an explanation.

'Oh, you're sure to do that,' said the cat, 'if only you walk long enough.'

Lewis Carroll

PLANNING

TASK ANALYSIS

THREE KEY QUESTIONS FOR ALL MEETINGS

- Who called the meeting?
  (This will establish who feels they own the issue)

- What do they want from the meeting?

- Where should the meeting be held?

PLANNING

TASK ANALYSIS
DESCRIBING THE ISSUE

Explore the following statements and questions to establish the *gap* between where you are now and where you want to be. These are:

- Task headline (language like 'How to...' or 'I wish...' encourages results-focused future thinking and specificity)

- Background history (just enough to stimulate ideas, not to drag people into the hole)

- Why is it an issue?

- Power and willingness to act

- What has already been tried and thought of?

- What would be an ideal solution - a *wish*? (imagine you have a magic wand and have a wish; often your wish is already someone else's solution being put into practice)

PLANNING

BACKWARD FORWARD PLANNING

STEPS BACKWARD

This is a planning tool. It is designed to help you identify the real issue you may wish to work on, often not easy to do in complex confusing organisations. Identifying the task also allows you to properly identify the problem owner. In turn, this tells you who to involve in the meeting, who not to involve and the type of meeting you should design.

- Form a starting *How to...* headline and write it down in the centre of the page

  How to create a new market for our products

- Say to yourself, 'Imagine we have now solved this problem...' (cover up the *How to...* and turn the problem statement into a solution)

  Create a new market for our products

- Then ask, 'What problem does that resolve for us...?' and write the answer down as a *How to...* headline

  How to sell more goods

BACKWARD FORWARD PLANNING

STEPS BACKWARD (Cont'd)

- With this new *How to...* headline ask the question again: 'Imagine we have now solved this problem (*how to sell more goods*), what problem does that resolve for us...?' Write the new answer as a *How to...* headline.

    How to increase sales

- Use this process three more times so that you now have five new *How to...* headlines

Increase sales	Problem solved would be	*How to achieve my targets*
Achieve my targets	Problem solved would be	*How to get my bonus*
Get my bonus	Problem solved would be	*How to pay off my loans*

BACKWARD FORWARD PLANNING

STEPS FORWARD

- Go back to your **original** headline and ask the question: 'Imagine we have now solved this problem (*how to create a new market for our products*), what else could it give us…?' or 'What more could we have…?' or 'What other benefits are there…?'. List at least three. They need to be different from the *backward* headlines.

> *New niches*
> *Keep our jobs*
> *Beat the competition*

- Put *How to…* in front of each of the benefits

> *How to find new niches*
> *How to keep our jobs*
> *How to beat the competition*

With the backward five, you now have eight headlines.

BACKWARD FORWARD PLANNING

STEPS FORWARD (Cont'd)

- The final question is a confronting question. Go back again to the **original** headline and ask: 'What is stopping us from making it happen?' and ' Why haven't we solved it?'. Write the answer down as a *How to…* headline

  How to do the market research

- Now look through all the headlines and decide which is the most appropriate starting point. It may be the original headline, which is fine as it will be chosen with some perspective

IMPORTANT TASKS vs THE MERELY URGENT
A MATRIX FOR DECIDING PRIORITIES

Using the diagram on the next page let's now look at *importance versus urgency*. Many of us go through our lives doing all the urgent things and never get to deal with the important issues. Often, eliminating one important issue also deals with numerous urgent ones.

Big bombs on short fuses are important and urgent. Big bombs on long fuses are important and less urgent, etc. Put your problems in the boxes and then decide. Be ruthless, as you probably do not have time to work on everything.

The diagram also lists *risk versus pay-off*. Having assigned the tasks for importance think about the consequence of success and the consequence of not solving the problem. Use this to tune your decision about what to work on.

IMPORTANT TASKS vs THE MERELY URGENT
A MATRIX FOR DECIDING PRIORITIES

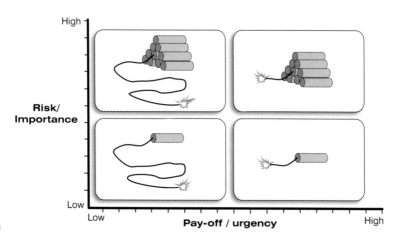

STRUCTURES FOR
PROBLEM SOLVING MEETINGS

USE A MAP

You can assume that at some point a problem solving meeting will get stuck and will feel directionless. If it were going to be that easy you would not have a problem!

Having a map helps you to avoid getting lost. It is also useful if the people helping you are starting to panic, because you can use it to reassure them that the meeting is on track.

In particular, a structure is vital where you want to use creative problem solving. Creativity, by definition, means you will be talking *non-sense* during parts of the meeting. If you are not, you are not discussing anything new!

The trouble with non-sense is that it **is** non-sense. It is not rational. How then do you use and navigate your way through irrational stuff?

Use a map designed for the purpose!

NINE-STEP SYNECTICS PROBLEM SOLVING PROCESS

Use this nine-step model if you are starting out to problem solve with no ideas as yet. A detailed description of the meaning of the parts and ways to use these follows in the next section, *How to use the nine-step model.*

1. Task Headline
2. Task Analysis
3. Springboards
4. Selection
5. Ways and Means
6. Emerging Idea
7. Itemised Response
8. Possible Solution
9. Next Step

BEST CURRENT THINKING: SHARING INTENTION & WINNING COMMITMENT

Sharing intention is appropriate when you have a suggestion or proposed solution that involves other people in its implementation. That is, you have a solution; other people have some or all of the responsibility for action.

- Present your proposal/suggestion to those involved
  - state how fixed it is (to what extent it can be modified by the group)

- Check they understand it
  - take questions for clarification
  - ask people to paraphrase key parts

- Evaluate it open-mindedly (using an itemised response)
  - everyone lists all possible benefits or pluses for the suggestion
  - everyone lists the problems or concerns they have, particularly ones that affect them personally

STRUCTURES FOR PROBLEM SOLVING MEETINGS

BEST CURRENT THINKING: SHARING INTENTION & WINNING COMMITMENT

- Prioritise the concerns
  - everyone selects two concerns they think need to be resolved first

- Take each concern in turn and problem solve it
  - ownership passes temporarily to the person who raised the concern (to avoid someone sitting in the meeting raising concerns for others to work on) before, finally, ownership returns to the ultimate owner of the meeting
  - the temporary problem owner, with the group's help, generates and develops ideas until the concern is resolved

- Modify or add to your original proposal
  - to take account of the new ideas
  - making sure that you (the original client) are still comfortable with the overall proposal

Repeat until the major concerns are resolved and the modified proposal meets everybody's needs.

NOTES

How to use
THE NINE-STEP MODEL

USE AS APPROPRIATE

I use the analogy of having a turbo charged car when writing about this model.
A turbo charged car is very powerful and this power is useful sometimes, for quick
overtaking in a limited road space for example. It is inappropriate to drive using the full
power all the time.

USE AS APPROPRIATE

The nine-step model is a complete creative problem solving tool that allows you to manage the energy and creativity of any group of people. Sometimes you may not need or wish to be especially creative, you just want to open your thinking a little and get a quick result.

Fine. Use the model as much as you need it. The underlying structure of your session or meeting will not change. The degree of creativity you apply can.

HOW TO USE THE NINE-STEP MODEL

TASK ANALYSIS

Earlier in the planning section I described a structure for task analysis and also discussed the need for information.

You can always add information; you cannot take it away once it is given.

Rather than waste time fully briefing people it is often better to get on with ideas after a minimal briefing. To solve problems you need ideas, not discussion around the issue. If you need more information as the session moves on you can always add it in. Remember the man in the hole earlier; don't let yourself get dragged in.

Often the original information is irrelevant to the final solution, so providing it just wastes time. There is no right or wrong to this, just be aware of how you are using time and for what purpose.

HOW TO USE THE NINE-STEP MODEL

TASK ANALYSIS

Task Headline
1

From problem owner starting "How to...

Task Analysis
2

From problem owner stating:
- Why problem/opportunity
- Brief background
- What have you tried/thought of
- Power to implement solution
- Dream solution
- Desired outcome of this meeting

Springboards
3

Beginning thoughts/ideas on how to approach problem from problem owner + group. starting "I wish..." or "How to..."

Selection
4

By problem owner on intrigue and appeal

SPRINGBOARDS

People took photographs for many years and accepted that you have to wait before you can see the prints. It took the daughter of Lands, inventor of the Polaroid camera, to ask (as only a child can) why she couldn't have the picture now.

'Why not', he thought, and began to consider how to make this possible.

Every new idea or problem solved begins with someone dreaming about a possibility. Until you have acknowledged the possibility you have no basis upon which to have ideas to take you on your journey.

Springboards

Beginning thoughts/ideas on how to approach problem from problem owner + group, starting "I wish..." or "How to..."

SPRINGBOARDS

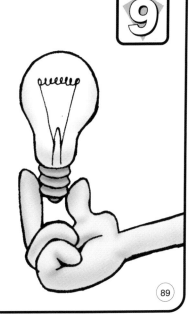

Springboards are the beginning thoughts that lead us to new thinking.

Ideas are specific and actionable thoughts that allow us to move towards possible solutions.

When Edison was working on the problem of inventing a light bulb he tried over 6000 different experiments using different materials for the filament, until he found success.

Einstein said, 'Imagination is more important than knowledge'. Springboarding is a technique for imagining. Einstein also said, 'If an idea is not at first absurd there is no hope for it'. Absurd ideas are the beginning of turning imagination into reality.

Springboard when you need newness.

HOW TO USE THE NINE-STEP MODEL

SPRINGBOARDS

- Springboarding is turbo-charged brainstorming
- Suspend judgement
- Rather than ask questions, have ideas; and if you don't know just guess
- Use the *in-out listening* process to stimulate ideas, but do not evaluate those ideas
- Try to avoid the self-censor that we all have in our minds
- Use *headlines* followed by *background* to express the springboards when working in a group
- Capture the headlines on flipcharts so that the group can revel in their productivity
- Use language like:
  - *How to ...,* or
  - *I wish...*

  Both of these formats encourage positive thinking about possible new futures

EXCURSION, JOURNEYS INTO ABSURDITY USING IMAGING, METAPHOR & ANALOGY

Springboarding, providing you truly suspend judgement, will lead to many novel perspectives and new ideas. Keep to the language of *I wish...* and *How to...* to encourage this.

Some of your potential for ideas will be tapped and you can do even better!

Recall a time when you were doing one thing and had ideas about another. This often happens when walking the dog, washing the car, in the shower, etc.

A process called *excursion* can be used to replicate this capacity of your subconscious to work on problems for itself without you even knowing it is happening.

91

EXCURSION, JOURNEYS INTO ABSURDITY USING IMAGING, METAPHOR & ANALOGY

There are many types of excursion and you can invent as many more as you wish. They share a common structure.

- Generate some thoughts and material **irrelevant** to the task

- Focus on this new thinking and allow it to suggest new springboards

  (They do not have to be connected to the task; this is not a rational process)

- If you are using the excursion in the latter part of the problem solving process, during idea development, use this material to invent absurd connections between the irrelevant material and the task

Remember that you are suspending judgement throughout this activity, so the notion of *silly* or *ridiculous* is not relevant. These are just thoughts.

If you are still unsure, you might find this interesting: when doctors examined Einstein's brain after his death they discovered it had many more synapses than a normal brain. It could make more connections faster than average. The suggestion is that it is this ability to make connections that makes people creative.

EXCURSION, JOURNEYS INTO ABSURDITY USING IMAGING, METAPHOR & ANALOGY

Benefits of absurdity:
- Introduces new and unusual perspectives
- Increases the amount of different data considered with the problem
- Helps people overcome the temptation to censor their thoughts

Examples:
- Cut up the ice cap and melt it to eliminate the Sahara desert
- Remove all my clothes in the meeting to demonstrate openness
- Insert a robot into the vein and program it to operate as necessary

EXCURSION, JOURNEYS INTO ABSURDITY USING IMAGING, METAPHOR & ANALOGY

Characteristics of an absurd idea:

Once in a lifetime	Impossible	Impractical	Expensive
Without conscience	Surprising	Fun	Highly risky
Violates some basic law of the universe, society or the company	Illogical	Shocking	Illegal
	Unconventional	Outrageous	

There are no rules about the right way to use absurd connections and ideas. They may have some element that directly addresses the problem - and they may have no connection at all!

On the following pages are outline descriptions of some excursions, just to get you started. Then go and invent some others for yourself. Some will work, others may not. It does not matter. There is no limit to how many you can use.

Examples:

- Buy everyone in the world a computer
- Sell the company to the union
- Just run over all the people, saves journey time and reduces population
- Dress the Board up as pantomime characters

HOW TO USE THE NINE-STEP MODEL

EXCURSION, JOURNEYS INTO ABSURDITY USING IMAGING, METAPHOR & ANALOGY

Imaging excursion

Additional rules for suspending judgement:

1. Keep the image visual - speak in pictures, ie: what you see, not describing a conversation
2. Keep it in one frame - imagine a cinema screen and create a composite image
3. Keep yourself out - if you put yourself in the picture you will immediately want to make it more rational

Process:

- Choose a word for the group, ideally one that can be ambiguous, and is not related to the issue, eg: steak/stake, plane/plain (do not spell it out to the group!)
- Do not write it down
- Allow the group 5-10 seconds and then ask someone to describe their first thoughts as a picture, what they see, not as a radio play
- Get participants to add in their first thoughts in turn
- Ask someone to make something extraordinary happen
- Have the group replay in their minds the image created and make their own notes
- Use this material to trigger additional speculation

EXCURSION, JOURNEYS INTO ABSURDITY USING IMAGING, METAPHOR & ANALOGY

Career excursion

- Allocate each member of the group a career or role
- Ask participants to think themselves into the role and make notes about thoughts that arise
  - either use this material directly to trigger new springboards
  - or have each participant talk to the group about their thoughts to trigger additional material and then get new springboards
- To build on this in a fun way, have the group play-act the roles when giving the springboards

EXCURSION, JOURNEYS INTO ABSURDITY USING IMAGING, METAPHOR & ANALOGY

Examples of career excursions: builder, diver, pilot, surgeon
>I wish I could build it up gradually, one brick at a time
>I wish I could breathe new life into the people
>I wish I could see the problem from a higher perspective like when I am flying
>I wish I could just cut out the bad bits

Or try Mickey Mouse, Charlie Chaplin, Richard Branson
>How to draw the plan like a fairy story
>I wish I could stop everyone tripping over their feet
>How to buy a company that can do it for us

EXCURSION, JOURNEYS INTO ABSURDITY USING IMAGING, METAPHOR & ANALOGY

Analogy excursion

- Participants should imagine becoming a part of an inanimate or live object
- Ask them to describe to the group how it feels and their relationship with others
- Use the material to trigger new springboards

Example

A group who had a problem on a bottling line became parts of the line. Each described the sensation of moving the bottle along, filling it, then capping it, etc. As the group explored the line in this way it became apparent why so many breakages were happening, one reason being that it is a *blind* system that cannot see. Now an electronic eye monitors a key part of the line.

EXCURSION, JOURNEYS INTO ABSURDITY USING IMAGING, METAPHOR & ANALOGY

Outside excursion

- Send the group outside and ask them to find something that intrigues or appeals to them

- Tell them to make notes about it and share this material on returning to the room to use as new triggers

- Alternatively, participants can bring a range of objects back into the room and place them in the middle as triggers

- If you want to be high-tech, give everyone a Polaroid camera and put the photos on a wall, using this as trigger material, or they could use a digital camera and project the pictures onto a screen

EXCURSION, JOURNEYS INTO ABSURDITY USING IMAGING, METAPHOR & ANALOGY

Example excursion

- Ask the problem owner to identify the essence of the need in order to make progress
- Ask the group to give you examples of this need from two worlds unrelated to the problem
- List examples on a flipchart
- Ask the group to use the examples to trigger new springboards

Example
The problem owner says, 'My key need is to recruit a specialist member of staff'. You might suggest, 'It sounds like you are trying to find very narrow cracks.'.

The group then list examples of finding narrow cracks in the worlds of science and mountaineering. In mountaineering, an example might be taking off your boots and climbing with your socks on, to become more sensitized to the rock.

The group look at the attributes of this example and how it can be linked to the problem under discussion, to give new perspectives to the thinking.

SELECTION

Generating springboards is fun and can contribute to a problem solving group really freeing their minds.

At some point you will need to move on in order to develop ideas and get to action. Sometimes actual solutions appear amongst the springboards. If this is the case you can shortcut the meeting, allow the problem owner to make his/her choices and finish.

When this happens it can be a blessing and makes selection easy. The downside is you may simply be choosing what you know without exploring other options fully.

Selection

By problem owner on intrigue and appeal

Does problem owner literally know how to do this?

NO   YES – go to Step 6
              (Emerging Idea)

Ways and Means

SELECTION

EVALUATION PROCESSES, A WARNING!

Evaluation is an interesting part of the process of making progress that begins with selection. New ideas and new ways often need new methods of measurement.

I know of two evaluation processes in current use, labelled *Stage-gates* and *Funnels and Gates*. I am not passing a general opinion on these processes, the names of which give a clue as to the intended use. *Stage-gates* is a way of managing a project where checks are made and an evaluation stage (gate) used to give a *go* or *no go* decision. *Funnels and Gates* is a similar idea using the concept of a funnel in the early part of the project to allow wide thinking and using more robust gates as the project progresses.

In my experience, most of the companies using these processes use the gate as a barrier to shut down thinking.

Be careful to avoid designing evaluation processes based upon the current operational world. Often these are irrelevant to new thinking, hence the itemised response described earlier as a way to treat new ideas gently.

SELECTION

OPENNESS TO INVENTING THE MEASURES

Key performance indicators (KPIs) can be a useful way to focus on achievement of goals, assuming you have identified useful KPIs.

In the case of creativity and innovation be aware that you need to focus on measuring the right thing. Lord Kelvin was quoted as saying that heavier-than-air machines would never fly. I imagine that in his mind he was measuring weight. Of course, what you actually need to measure is lift.

In new product development workshops people are often desperate to *cluster* the new ideas. This usually means applying the existing segmentation to new thinking, whereupon a lot of the novelty is lost because the old assumptions and past experience get dragged in together with the old label.

SELECTION

SELECTION BASED UPON INTRIGUE

A typical selection process after brainstorming is to go through all the ideas ticking the ones that appear useful and deleting the ones you do not understand.

This *good idea, bad idea* approach looks to apply instant reason to an unreasonable process (springboarding) and is completely the wrong way to proceed.

Intrigue is a notion of considering a springboard and imagining where your thoughts might take you if you explored them in more detail. This is the selection criteria recommended, particularly when you wish for novelty and newness.

It is only possible if you have an **ideas development** process to follow it. This will be described shortly.

SELECTION BASED UPON INTRIGUE

WHAT IS INTRIGUE?

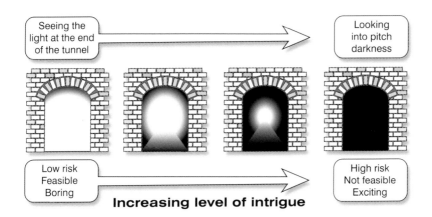

Seeing the light at the end of the tunnel

Looking into pitch darkness

Low risk
Feasible
Boring

High risk
Not feasible
Exciting

Increasing level of intrigue

SELECTION BASED UPON INTRIGUE

EXPLORING TUNNELS

When you can see the light at the end of the tunnel, you know where it goes. It is a journey you know about, taking you somewhere familiar.

If you choose a springboard in this tunnel you are unlikely to innovate.

Dark tunnels lead to the unknown and you will not know what is there unless you go on the journey to explore. A black hole could lead somewhere exciting or could be a brick wall. The only way to find out is to travel the path.

Springboards in this tunnel are *intriguing*. They are exciting because they go into the unknown. It is risky, and the journey lacks feasibility because you do not know yet where you are going.

This tunnel **may** lead you to new and innovative possible solutions.

SELECTION BASED UPON INTRIGUE

EXPLORING OFF THE TRACK

Another way to conceptualise intrigue is to imagine going for a walk in a beautiful country estate garden.

You may see pathways that lead to places in front of your eyes and as you wander down them new vistas open up. You may leave the paths and wander into woods or up hills to explore new areas, feeling nervous, perhaps, about getting lost but also excited about what else you may find.

Another analogy is the off-piste skier, leaving the marked track and exploring new parts of the mountain. This is often nerve-racking and exciting, but you find new paths by doing it.

Intrigue is a vital step in the **creative** problem solving process. Give time to allow review of the springboards and become intrigued. You have to play with the thoughts and let them develop. Intrigue sometimes just happens, and sometimes you need to let your mind mull things over for a while.

IDEA DEVELOPMENT

CREATE RATIONAL SOLUTIONS FROM NON-SENSE

Selection based upon intrigue is what has allowed you to choose something irrational that looks like it might be fun or scary. It has no sense, no meaning, no direction, yet!

It is just intriguing!

Idea development is a structured process for taking non-sense and gradually developing sense until you achieve rational actionable possible solutions.

You cannot guarantee this every time but more often than not you will achieve something useful if you follow the process described.

I use a metaphor to describe the idea development process.

9

IDEA DEVELOPMENT
CREATE RATIONAL SOLUTIONS FROM NON-SENSE

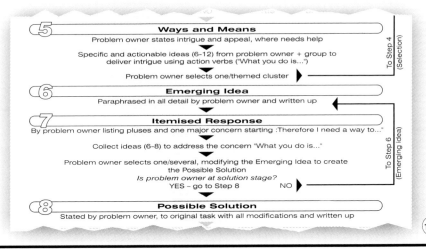

IDEA DEVELOPMENT

CREATE RATIONAL SOLUTIONS FROM NON-SENSE

Playing snowballs (or, it is all just balls)

I mentioned snowflakes earlier. I use this as a metaphor for the idea development process. This is like catching snowflakes and creating snowballs. Each snowflake is unique and beautiful. If you simply clap your hands on to it, it will melt leaving you with nothing. In the beginning you must treat the snowflakes gently and pat them into place, gradually creating a snowball. As it forms it becomes more robust and you can begin to apply more pressure.

You can continue to add snowflakes for ever so your snowball has infinite size, and an infinite number of forms as you choose where to add the next snowflakes. It will become as hard as glacial ice, hard and very robust. Eventually you could even choose to roll it down the mountain and let it have a life of its own.

IDEA DEVELOPMENT

CREATE RATIONAL SOLUTIONS FROM NON-SENSE

The role of the problem owner is to give direction to the group. The problem owner has a key role here, ie: describing his or her early thoughts even though these still may be quite irrational. It is normal to be in a creative fog at this point, which is why you have a map, the nine-step model, to follow.

Idea development is often tough, like wading through a swamp, having to watch out for crocodiles. The key steps are:

- Work with one springboard at a time - you can always go back and try others later
- The problem owner talks to the group about the intrigue, and the group uses in-out listening to trigger specific and actionable ideas that could deliver the intrigue

HOW TO USE THE NINE-STEP MODEL

IDEA DEVELOPMENT

CREATE RATIONAL SOLUTIONS FROM NON-SENSE

Specific and actionable ideas use a headline format like: *What you do is ......*.

During springboarding your thinking was divergent. A selection has now been made and the use of specific and actionable ideas is a structured approach to beginning to invent and create something that has rationality and feasibility.

1. The group generates a series of specific and actionable ideas, fewer of them than for springboards; the problem owner should join in and give ideas as well

2. Stop after a while and invite the problem owner to consider the ideas to see if **one or more of them is beginning to suggest a concept or direction of thinking that could be pursued further**

IDEA DEVELOPMENT

CREATE RATIONAL SOLUTIONS FROM NON-SENSE

3. If *no*, continue to get more ideas; use an excursion if you wish to keep the thinking open-minded

4. If *yes*, get the problem owner to use an itemised response (see following pages) to identify the pluses, as well as one major concern. (Work through one concern at a time. The danger of raising too many concerns too soon for a new idea is that the group become so de-energised they give up hope.)

5. Collect ideas to address the concern and then go back to the problem owner and repeat the process from Step 2

6. Keep cycling through the process until you get to a solution, or decide it is going nowhere. If the latter, try another springboard

HOW TO USE THE NINE-STEP MODEL

IDEA DEVELOPMENT

CREATE RATIONAL SOLUTIONS FROM NON-SENSE

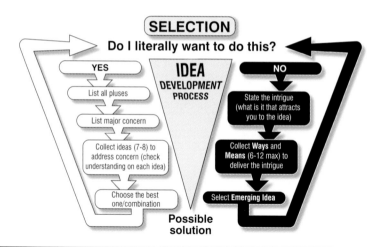

SELECTION

Do I literally want to do this?

IDEA DEVELOPMENT PROCESS

YES
- List all pluses
- List major concern
- Collect ideas (7-8) to address concern (check understanding on each idea)
- Choose the best one/combination

NO
- State the intrigue (what is it that attracts you to the idea)
- Collect **Ways** and **Means** (6-12 max) to deliver the intrigue
- Select **Emerging Idea**

Possible solution

IDEA DEVELOPMENT

CREATE RATIONAL SOLUTIONS FROM NON-SENSE

Consider the following example:

My problem is: *How to keep the leaves off the railway line.*

The springboard I have chosen is: *I wish you could tie cleaning men and women to the train and give them a scrubbing brush.*

A specific and actionable idea to address this is: *What you do is use convicts.*
This would solve my problem.

List all the pluses for this idea.

There are many… for example: I like the idea of dealing with the prison overpopulation, many would not survive!

IDEA DEVELOPMENT
CREATE RATIONAL SOLUTIONS FROM NON-SENSE

Using absurd thinking

My major concern is: how to be more humane. I need, therefore, a way to achieve the effect of unlimited supply. Give me some further ideas.

- Put lavatory brushes on the front
- Put a road sweeping truck on rails in front of the train
- Stick car ice scrapers on the train

These are looking good, nothing illegal here and they will all solve the problem.

I like the scraping concept. My major concern is: how to scrape hard enough.

- Put metal scrapers on the front
- Use a laser beam instead
- Use sound to vibrate the goo to make it softer

This is a contrived illustration to try and get a difficult concept across. You will see how a ludicrous suggestion like using cleaners, treated positively using an itemised response, can help to generate more feasible ideas. (Someone has built a working model using a laser!)

IDEA DEVELOPMENT

CREATE RATIONAL SOLUTIONS FROM NON-SENSE

Possible solution(s)

It is important to keep the problem solving going until you get actionable solutions. I use the plural here because it can be helpful to have alternative solutions. In the beginning when writing about risk I introduced the idea of framing your activity as an experiment to give you permission to fail.

James Dyson tried around 2000 versions of his dual cyclone before going ahead to manufacturing. I use the expression *possible solution* because new ideas are often untested and need to be given a chance to see what happens. Refer back to the itemised response regarding this. Be careful of picking away at your possible solution until it ceases to have any value. Certain UK supermarkets are way in front of the rest. They have tried many new ideas, some of which worked, and some did not. The culture of some of the other supermarkets is geared more to analysing and making sure their new ideas are perfect. They never are, of course, so they try fewer new things. The result is obvious!

NEXT STEPS

Seems obvious but most problem solving fails because the energy and enthusiasm generated during the fun bit, solving the problem, quickly evaporate when reality hits.

⑨ **Next Step**

Actions listed by problem owner: what, by whom, by when

NEXT STEPS

USE SMART

Use SMART criteria to describe the next steps you are going to take to start putting your solution into practice.

Specific - They should be described in such a way that you can imagine walking out of the door and taking the action.

Measurable - Take time to decide how you will measure success. If the idea is very new be prepared to invent a way to measure it. New measures for very novel ideas may be vague in the beginning. Do not fall into the trap of measuring something new with measures designed for something old. (On the principle that a stone is too heavy to fly then so is an aeroplane.)

Accountable - This connects with problem ownership. Avoid groupthink. New things usually need someone with the energy and drive to make them happen. Accountability provides the focus for this and also gives that person permission to step outside the norm of the day to day.

Realistic - For something to happen you have to be able to do something. Make sure you problem solve far enough to get real.

NEXT STEPS

USE SMART (Cont'd)

Time bound - Time is a resource. When the money runs out it is obvious and projects stop. Time tends to be treated as limitless. Set lots of short-term goals. People cannot manage long-term ones, they seem so far away there is no urgency to complete the task until it is too late.

AND FINALLY

You can never know you will succeed when you begin to problem solve. What you can do is raise the probability of success.

You will do this by establishing the best climate you can, by getting the right people involved in the right ways, by following a map to navigate your way through the difficult times, by focusing on having ideas rather than debating in circles, by experimenting with possible solutions so that you learn.

In this book you have the tools to help you do all of these things. Have fun and enjoy your success. Keep the failures in perspective, get up and try again.

About the Author

Jonne Ceserani
Managing Director, Power & Grace.
Jonne is a coach, facilitator and trainer who regularly uses the tools described in this book when working with his clients.

He works around the world developing and delivering creativity, innovation, change, leadership and coaching programmes. His range of clients is diverse and has included Walkers Snack Foods, Barclays Bank, BAA, Coca-Cola, Diageo, O2 and Unilever.

He has a degree in Management Science from UMIST, where he focused on Industrial Psychology and Organisational Development. He is a Neuro Linguistic Programming master practitioner.

He worked with the DuPont company for 10 years, managing corporate finance teams, as an international auditor, and as a project manager introducing a number of change programmes into the IT division. All of these roles involved problem solving.

Jonne is the author of *Big ideas, putting the zest into creativity and innovation at work*, a leadership book that describes how to introduce innovation programmes into an organisation. Jonne lives in the peak district on the borders of the national park where he and his wife Tricia enjoy looking after their woodland and exploring the many walks in the area.

Jonne can be contacted at: jonne@powerandgrace.co.uk

THE MANAGEMENT POCKETBOOK SERIES

Pocketbooks

Appraisals
Assertiveness
Balance Sheet
Business Planning
Business Writing
Call Centre Customer Care
Career Transition
Challengers
Coaching
Communicator's
Competencies
Controlling Absenteeism
Creative Manager's
C.R.M.
Cross-cultural Business
Cultural Gaffes
Customer Service
Decision-making
Developing People
Discipline
Diversity
E-commerce
Emotional Intelligence
Employment Law
Empowerment

Energy and Well-being
Facilitator's
Flexible Workplace
Handling Complaints
Icebreakers
Impact & Presence
Improving Efficiency
Improving Profitability
Induction
Influencing
International Trade
Interviewer's
I.T. Trainer's
Key Account Manager's
Leadership
Learner's
Manager's
Managing Budgets
Managing Cashflow
Managing Change
Managing Recruitment
Managing Upwards
Managing Your Appraisal
Marketing
Meetings

Mentoring
Motivation
Negotiator's
Networking
NLP
Openers & Closers
People Manager's
Performance Management
Personal Success
Positive Mental Attitude
Presentations
Problem Behaviour
Problem Solving
Project Management
Quality
Resolving Conflict
Sales Excellence
Salesperson's
Self-managed Development
Starting In Management
Strategy
Stress
Succeeding at Interviews
Teambuilding Activities
Teamworking

Telephone Skills
Telesales
Thinker's
Time Management
Trainer Standards
Trainer's
Training Evaluation
Training Needs Analysis
Virtual Teams
Vocal Skills

Pocketsquares

Great Training Robbery
Hook Your Audience

Pocketfiles

Trainer's Blue Pocketfile of
Ready-to-use Activities

Trainer's Green Pocketfile of
Ready-to-use Activities

Trainer's Red Pocketfile of
Ready-to-use Activities

27.2.06

ORDER FORM

Your details

Name _____

Position _____

Company _____

Address _____

_____

_____

Telephone _____

Fax _____

E-mail _____

VAT No. (EC companies) _____

Your Order Ref _____

Please send me:

No.
copies

The Problem Solving Pocketbook ☐

The _____ Pocketbook ☐

The _____ Pocketbook ☐

The _____ Pocketbook ☐

The _____ Pocketbook ☐

Order by Post
MANAGEMENT POCKETBOOKS LTD
LAUREL HOUSE, STATION APPROACH,
ALRESFORD, HAMPSHIRE SO24 9JH UK
Order by Phone, Fax or Internet
Telephone: +44 (0)1962 735573
Facsimile: +44 (0)1962 733637
E-mail: sales@pocketbook.co.uk
Web: www.pocketbook.co.uk

MANAGEMENT POCKETBOOKS